WINTER STEWS & ONE-POT DINNERS

WINTER
STEWS &
ONE-POT
DINNERS

TASTY RECIPES THAT FILL YOUR
BELLY AND WARM YOUR HEART

DANIELLA MALFITANO

THE COUNTRYMAN PRESS

A DIVISION OF W. W. NORTON & COMPANY

INDEPENDENT PUBLISHERS SINCE 1923

TO MY SWEETHEART.
JUST AS FOOD AND COOKING MAKE ME DO
THE HAPPY DANCE, YOU DO THAT TO MY HEART.
YOU GIVE MY LIFE JOY AND MEANING.
THANK YOU FOR YOUR CONSTANT
LOVE AND SUPPORT.

CONTENTS

Introduction

Finally, a cookbook dedicated to the casual cooking and common recipes of the home cook! Nothing says home cooking more than stews and casseroles, right? They are some of the most comforting dishes that we eat and enjoy, and can be prepared easily in the home kitchen. For many of us, these dishes will elicit vivid childhood memories—memories of days gone by, and of being taken care of by others, especially our loved ones. These are the recipes that give our life much joy and meaning.

I hope you will find Winter Stews & Casseroles to be a rich and soul-warming addition to the Best Ever cookbook series. This cookbook includes fifty deliciously timeless recipes, ranging from Classic Chicken and Fish Dishes to Hearty Beef Dishes, and Irresistible Pork and Lamb Dishes to Flavorful Vegetable and Side Dishes. You might see recipes that you grew up making or eating, and recipes you simply might have just forgotten about over time that are waiting to be remembered again. The recipes contained in this book are simple to make and approachable for all types of cooks and all levels of cooking skill, so fear not! Anyone and everyone can make these recipes, and it is my hope that you will! Every recipe in this book is fun to make, delicious to enjoy, and a perfect addition to your cooking repertoire. Dig in and let these recipes transport you to the days of yore.

Enjoy!

With pleasure and an appetite,
Chef Daniella Malfitano

CHAPTER ONE

CLASSIC CHICKEN & FISH DISHES

Chicken & Vegetable Stew

This is a delicious and hearty chicken stew with all of the traditional fixings, as well as the addition of sweet corn and red bell pepper to brighten it up a bit. This recipe uses chicken thighs, but you can use breasts or tenders if you prefer white meat instead. This doesn't take long to make and can be a nice dinner any day of the week.

Serves 6–8

2 tablespoons butter

1 tablespoon olive oil

3½ pounds boneless skinless chicken thighs, diced

3 teaspoons salt, divided

2 teaspoons black pepper, divided

3 cups water

1 cup onion, finely diced

1 red bell pepper, chopped

3 teaspoons thyme

3 teaspoons poultry seasoning

4 small potatoes, chopped

2 stalks celery, chopped

1 cup frozen peas

1 cup frozen corn

1½ cups chicken broth

¼ cup all-purpose flour

Add the butter and oil to a stockpot and heat to medium. Add the chicken to the pot, season it with 2 teaspoons of salt and 1 teaspoon of pepper and sear each piece just to brown.

Next, add the water, onion, bell pepper, thyme, poultry seasoning, and the remaining salt and pepper, and bring the mixture to a boil over medium-high heat. Once it boils, reduce the heat and add the potatoes and celery. Cover the pot and simmer for 35 minutes or until the chicken and vegetables are cooked through.

Lastly, add the peas and corn and cook for 5 minutes. In a bowl, whisk together the chicken broth and flour until no lumps remain, then gradually pour it into the stew while whisking. Simmer the stew on medium heat until it begins to thicken, and then turn off the heat. Taste and adjust the seasonings as needed before serving.

Creamy Chicken Casserole

Cream cheese gives this dish a smooth and creamy finish that will leave you wanting more. You can make this with any type of noodle you'd like, to mix it up from time to time. Enjoy this alone as a satisfying meal or with salad on the side.

Serves 8–10

2 boneless, skinless chicken breasts

3 teaspoons salt, divided

1½ teaspoons black pepper, divided

4 tablespoons butter, divided

1 tablespoon olive oil

1 small onion, diced

1½ cups carrots, diced

6 tablespoons flour

½ teaspoon thyme

½ teaspoon poultry seasoning

1 cup milk

3 cups chicken broth

4 ounces cream cheese

1 cup white cheddar cheese

16 ounces egg noodles

1½ cups frozen peas

¼ cup Parmesan cheese

¾ cup panko breadcrumbs

Preheat the oven to 350°F. Place two chicken breasts on a baking sheet and season with 1 teaspoon of salt and ½ teaspoon of pepper. Cook the chicken in the oven for 25 to 30 minutes, or until it's cooked through.

Begin making the rest of the casserole while the chicken cooks. Heat a stockpot to medium heat with 2 tablespoons of butter and the oil. Add the onion and carrots and cook for about 5 to 7 minutes. Next, whisk in the flour, thyme, poultry seasoning, and the remaining salt and pepper and cook an additional 2 minutes.

Gradually pour in the milk and broth and cook just until the mixture begins to boil. Turn off the heat and stir in the cream cheese and the white cheddar cheese until everything melts together. Cook the egg noodles in boiling salted water for 5 minutes, or until they are halfway cooked. While the noodles cook, cube the chicken breasts and add them to the stockpot. Then drain the noodles and add them to the stockpot, along with the peas. Fold everything together and then pour the casserole into a greased 9 x 13-inch baking pan. Make the topping by combining the last 2 tablespoons of butter with the Parmesan cheese and panko breadcrumbs and mix well, then sprinkle it over the top and bake the casserole in the oven for 30 minutes or until it is bubbling and the top is golden brown.

Chicken Tamale Casserole

This recipe is one that you'll love if you like the taste of corn muffins and enchiladas. The Monterey jack and cheddar cheeses go very well with the chicken, cumin, and green chilies. For more of a kick, you can try substituting pepper jack cheese.

Serves 8

1 cup shredded cheddar cheese, divided

½ cup milk

¼ cup liquid eggs

1 teaspoon ground cumin

1 can (15-ounce) creamed corn

1 box (8.5-ounce) corn muffin mix

1 can (4-ounce) chopped green chilies

1 jar (10-ounce) red enchilada sauce

3 cups cooked chicken, shredded

1 cup shredded Monterey Jack cheese

¼ cup cilantro, minced

Preheat the oven to 400°F. In a mixing bowl, combine ¼ cup of the cheddar cheese with the milk, liquid eggs, ground cumin, creamed corn, corn muffin mix, and green chilies and mix just until everything is well combined. Do not overmix or the base won't be as tender. Pour the mixture into a greased 9 x 13-inch casserole dish and bake for 15 minutes.

Using a fork, poke holes all over the base and then pour the enchilada sauce onto it. Layer the shredded chicken and then the Monterey Jack cheese and remaining cheddar cheese, sprinkled evenly over the top, and place it in the oven to bake for 15 minutes, just until it is bubbly and melted. Remove it from the oven and garnish it with cilantro before serving.

French-Style Chicken Stew

I learned this dish in school and had to make it several times in order to master this classic. No matter how many times I make it, I still love it. The chicken and smoky bacon work well together when bathed in the red wine sauce, and the mushrooms and pearl onions only make it better. Serve this as is in bowls or over mounds of mashed potatoes.

Serves 6

2 tablespoons olive oil

3 strips (4-ounce) thick cut bacon, cubed

8 pieces chicken thighs and legs

3 teaspoons salt, divided

2 teaspoons black pepper, divided

2 medium carrots, chopped

1 cup button mushrooms, sliced

1 cup pearl onions, peeled and left whole

2 cloves garlic, chopped

2½ cups red wine

1 cup chicken broth

5 sprigs thyme

2 tablespoons flour

1 tablespoon butter

Preheat the oven to 250°F. Heat the olive oil in a large cast iron pot or Dutch oven over medium heat, then add the bacon and brown for 5 minutes. Remove the bacon pieces to a paper towel–lined plate to drain, but leave the excess bacon fat at the bottom of the pot. You'll use it to cook the rest of the dish.

Heat the same pot over medium heat. While the pot heats up, season the chicken pieces with 2 teaspoons of salt and 1 teaspoon of pepper, then add the chicken to the pot and sear each piece on both sides, just to brown it quickly, keeping the center of the chicken raw to finish cooking later. After you have seared each piece of chicken, transfer the pieces to a plate and set them aside.

Heat the pot again to medium heat, adding a bit more oil if necessary. Then add the carrots, button mushrooms, and pearl onions and season with the remaining salt and pepper. Cook the vegetables for 10 minutes, then add the garlic and cook for 1 minute longer, gradually pouring in the wine while you scrape up all of the burned bits on the bottom of the pan to incorporate them into your sauce and give it a richer flavor. Gently add the bacon and chicken back to the pot, and then add the chicken broth and thyme. Bring this mixture to a boil, then cover the pot and simmer it on low heat for 35 to 40 minutes. Add the flour to a small bowl and then mix it with the butter and a splash of the stew liquid, mixing well to remove any lumps. Pour this mixture into the stew and continue to cook for 5 to 10 minutes or just until the mixture thickens and coats the back of a spoon. Serve each guest a piece or two of chicken, some sauce, and a good spoonful of the vegetables and bacon.

Tuna Noodle Casserole

I couldn't write this book without including the most classic casserole dish of all time: Tuna Noodle Casserole! This dish has been one of America's most loved casseroles since the 1950s. Instead of the traditional recipe that uses a can of soup as the sauce, this recipe will show you how to make a simple sauce from scratch.

Serves 6–8

7 ounces dried egg noodles

¼ cup plus 2 tablespoons butter, divided

¼ cup flour

¾ teaspoon garlic powder

1 teaspoon salt

½ teaspoon pepper

3¾ cups milk

½ cup Parmesan cheese

1 cup frozen peas

2 cans (6.5-ounce each) tuna, drained and flaked

⅓ cup coarse breadcrumbs

1 teaspoon thyme leaves

Preheat the oven to 350°F. In a large pot of boiling salted water, cook the egg noodles for 5 minutes, then drain and set them aside. Combine 2 tablespoons of butter and the flour, garlic powder, salt, and pepper in a pot over low heat and mix well. Gradually whisk in the milk and stir until the sauce just begins to thicken. Mix in the Parmesan cheese and remove pot from the heat.

Add the drained noodles, peas, and tuna and gently mix well. In a separate bowl, make the topping by mixing the breadcrumbs, the remaining butter, and the thyme. Pour the casserole into a greased 9 x 13-inch baking pan and sprinkle with topping. Bake for 18 to 20 minutes or until golden brown.

Chicken & Wild Rice Stew

This stew is perfect for a cold day when you just want something warm and nourishing. The wild rice and chicken work really well together and create a very fulfilling stew that will leave you happy and full. I like shredded chicken breasts here, but you can certainly add diced and cubed chicken bits if you prefer.

Serves 6

8 tablespoons butter, divided

½ cup chopped carrots

½ cup chopped celery

1 small yellow onion, chopped

4 cups chicken broth

2 cups water

2 large chicken breasts, cooked and shredded

¾ cup wild rice

2 teaspoons salt

½ teaspoon black pepper

1 teaspoon herbes de Provence

2 small bay leaves

½ cup all-purpose flour

2 cups milk

Heat a stockpot to medium heat and then add 2 tablespoons of butter and the carrots, celery, and onion and sauté for 5 to 7 minutes. Next, increase the heat to high and add the chicken broth, water, and shredded chicken pieces and mix well. Bring the stew to a boil and then add in the wild rice and cook for 5 minutes. Reduce the heat, add the salt, black pepper, herbes de Provence, and bay leaves to the pot, then cover and simmer the stew for 25 minutes.

While the stew cooks, heat a saucepan to low heat, whisk together the remaining butter and the flour, and cook for 2 minutes, stirring constantly. Gradually stir in the milk, whisking constantly to smooth out any lumps. Cook this mixture for approximately 5 minutes, just until it begins to thicken, and then remove it from the heat.

Once the rice mixture has finished cooking and the rice tastes tender, pour the milk mixture into the stew pot and stir just to combine. Continue to cook the stew for 10 to 15 minutes to thicken it, then taste it and adjust the seasonings as necessary before serving.

Tip: Herbes de Provence is a combination of classic French dried herbs and spices and can be found in the spice section of most supermarkets and specialty markets.

Old-Fashioned Chicken & Dumplings

If you're in the mood for a bone-sticking meal, then look no further. This recipe for chicken and dumplings is certainly delicious and made just like it should be. The chicken stew is thick and classic with onions, carrots, and peas while the dumplings are made from scratch and are deliciously enhanced with a bit of dried herbs.

Serves 8

5 tablespoons unsalted butter, divided

2 teaspoons olive oil

3½ pounds boneless chicken breasts

3½ teaspoons salt, divided

½ teaspoon black pepper, divided

1 small yellow onion, finely chopped

2 carrots, finely chopped

2 cups plus 2 tablespoons all-purpose flour, divided

1½ cups chicken broth

8 ounces egg noodles

1 cup frozen peas

2 teaspoons herbes de Provence

2 teaspoons baking powder

1 cup whole milk

Preheat the oven to 350°F. Heat a Dutch oven over medium heat, then add 3 tablespoons butter and all of the oil. Season the chicken with 2 teaspoons of salt and ¼ teaspoon of pepper and then add it to the pot and sear it on both sides, just to brown. Transfer the chicken to a plate and set it aside.

Add 1 tablespoon butter to the same pot and heat it to medium heat. Add the onion and carrots and cook for 10 minutes. Sprinkle 2 tablespoons of the flour into the pot and stir it into the vegetables for 5 more minutes, then gradually whisk in the broth, ½ teaspoon of salt, and ¼ teaspoon pepper. Add the chicken back to the pot and cook on medium-low, covered, for about 30 to 35 minutes or until the chicken is cooked through. Once the chicken is cooked, remove it from the pot and let it cool slightly.

While the chicken cools, cook the egg noodles in a large pot of boiling salted water for 5 minutes or until the noodles are halfway cooked, then drain them and fold them into the stew along with the frozen peas. Once the chicken is cool enough to touch, remove the skin, dice it into chunks, place back into the stew, and mix gently to combine.

Combine the remaining 2 cups of flour, the last teaspoon of salt, the herbes de Provence, and the baking powder in a large bowl. Melt the last tablespoon of butter, then add the milk and melted butter and mix just until the dough comes together. Drop heaping spoonfuls of dough, one by one, into the stew, leaving a bit of space between each dumpling. Cover the pot and place it in the oven to bake for 15 minutes, then uncover and bake for another 5 minutes to brown the dumplings.

Shrimp & Rice Casserole

Not only is this Shrimp and Rice Casserole deliciously flavored, it's also elegant-looking in the baking dish presented to your guests. The sauce has a ton of character from the garlic, cardamom, cinnamon, cumin, and chili powder, and the basmati rice is drizzled with a lemon turmeric liquid that ought to earn this dish a beauty award.

Serves 6

2 tablespoons olive oil

2 onions, finely chopped

1 tablespoon minced garlic

1 teaspoon garam masala

1½ pounds large raw shrimp, peeled, and deveined
(26 to 30 per pound)

1 teaspoon salt, divided

1 cup plain yogurt

1½ cups water

1 cup basmati rice

⅔ cup lemon juice

⅛ teaspoon turmeric

¼ teaspoon saffron threads

¼ bunch cilantro

Lime, sliced into wedges

Preheat the oven to 350°F. Heat a stock pot on medium heat with oil, then add the onions, garlic, and garam masala, and cook for 5 minutes. Add the shrimp to the pan, season with ½ teaspoon of salt, and cook, stirring frequently for 3 minutes, just until shrimp begin to turn pink around the edges. Reduce the heat to low, add the yogurt, and cook for 10 minutes, stirring occasionally.

Add the water and rice to a pot and bring to a boil. Cover the pot and cook the rice for 10 minutes, then drain and set it aside. Stir together the lemon juice, turmeric, and remaining salt; mix well and set aside.

Butter a 3½-quart casserole dish, then spread it with about ⅓ of the rice. Top the rice with the shrimp mixture and finish with the rest of the rice. Drizzle the lemon turmeric liquid over the rice and sprinkle evenly with saffron threads. Cover the dish tightly with foil and bake it in the oven for 15 to 20 minutes or until the rice is tender. Uncover the dish and serve warm right out of the oven with a garnish of cilantro and lime wedges.

Tip: Garam masala is a combination of classic Indian ground spices and can be found in the spice section of most supermarkets and specialty markets.

Chicken, Mushroom, & Pesto Casserole

There is something pretty spectacular about the combination of chicken, mushrooms, and pesto. If you have never tried this combo, I encourage you to make this the first. You won't be disappointed by how easy it is to make, and how utterly satisfying it tastes. The basil gives this dish a sweetish flavor that works wonders with the nuttiness of the mushrooms.

Serves 6

3 cups packed fresh basil

5 cloves garlic, divided

1 tablespoon lemon juice

1 teaspoon salt, divided

½ teaspoon black pepper, divided

⅓ cup pine nuts, toasted

½ cup grated Parmesan

½ cup olive oil

16 ounces penne pasta

¼ cup butter

1½ cups mushrooms, sliced

2 cups cooked chicken, diced

2 cups grated mozzarella cheese, divided

Preheat the oven to 350°F and begin by making the pesto. In a food processor, combine the basil, 3 garlic cloves, lemon juice, ½ teaspoon salt, ¼ teaspoon pepper, pine nuts, Parmesan cheese, and olive oil and pulse until the mixture is smooth. Season to taste and add more salt and pepper if necessary.

Fill a large stockpot with water and a big pinch of salt and bring it to a boil. Boil the pasta for 6 minutes, or just before it is completely finished cooking, then drain and pour it into a mixing bowl. Heat a large saucepan over medium heat with butter. Once the butter coats the pan, toss in the remaining garlic cloves and mushrooms and sauté until the mushrooms are tender (about 6 to 8 minutes), then add them to the mixing bowl with the pasta. Add the pesto, diced chicken, and 1 cup of grated mozzarella cheese to the pasta and gently fold everything together to combine.

Pour the pasta mixture into a buttered 9 x 13-inch casserole pan and sprinkle the top with the remaining mozzarella cheese. Bake for 15 minutes or until the cheese is melted and bubbly, then remove the casserole from the oven and serve hot.

Chicken Paprika

Delicious Chicken Paprika is one of those simple yet succulent dishes that nourishes your hungry taste buds when you need something filling. This dish comes together rather quickly in one pan and is the perfect recipe when you need a satisfying meal in no time. Serve this over rice or pasta for an even heartier dinner.

Serves 6

4 tablespoons butter

3 tablespoons paprika

1 medium yellow onion, finely chopped

4 chicken breasts, cubed

2 teaspoons salt

1 teaspoon black pepper

2 cups chicken broth

3 teaspoons water

2 teaspoons cornstarch

4 tablespoons sour cream

Heat a sauté pan to medium-high heat, then add the butter to melt. Add the paprika to the pan and stir for 1 minute. Next, add the onion to the pan and cook on medium-low for 10 minutes, or until the onion is tender.

Add the chicken to the pan and season it with salt and pepper. Cook the chicken for about 2 minutes, stirring frequently. Gradually add the chicken broth while scraping up any brown bits from the bottom of the pan. Bring this mixture to a quick boil, then turn the heat to low and simmer for 10 minutes, or until the chicken is fully cooked.

Combine the water and cornstarch in a cup and mix to make a smooth slurry, then immediately whisk it into the sauce. Continue to cook the sauce for 2 to 4 more minutes, or until it begins to thicken, then stir in the sour cream and remove it from the heat.

Spicy Shrimp Stew

The red pepper, paprika, and cumin make for a very flavorful broth for this Spicy Shrimp Stew. This recipe can be made mild, but if you're feeling like more heat add double the amount of red pepper flakes. It's important to use raw shrimp in this recipe in order to get a full-bodied broth that stands up to the rest of the ingredients.

Serves 4–6

3 tablespoons olive oil

2 cups yellow onion, finely chopped

6 cloves garlic, minced

½ cup carrot, finely chopped

1 russet potato, cubed small

½ teaspoon cayenne pepper, divided

½ teaspoon ground cumin, divided

½ teaspoon salt

¼ teaspoon pepper

1 bay leaf

1½ pounds raw medium/large shrimp, peeled and deveined (31 to 35 per pound)

¼ cup tomato paste

1¼ cups dry white wine

¼ cup water

3 tablespoons fresh lime juice

3 green onions, minced

Heat the oil in a large pot over medium heat. Add the onions and garlic and cook for 2 minutes. Next add the carrot and potato and continue to cook for 3 more minutes. Season the vegetables with ¼ teaspoon cayenne, ¼ teaspoon cumin, salt, pepper, and the bay leaf. Continue to cook for 10 minutes, or until all of the vegetables are tender.

While the vegetables finish cooking, season the raw shrimp with the remaining cayenne and cumin. Stir in the tomato paste and cook for 1 minute, then gradually pour in the white wine to deglaze while whisking up any brown bits from the bottom of the pot. Next add the water and lime juice and bring the stew to a simmer for 5 minutes. Add shrimp and let them cook for 5 minutes, or just until they turn pink. Spoon into bowls and garnish with green onions.

Moroccan Chicken Stew

You will be transported straight to Morocco in mere moments once you begin cooking this stew. Turmeric, cumin, coriander, cinnamon, ginger, and cayenne sing together to create a very warm flavor base for this stew, while the tomatoes and raisins add bright sweetness. The chickpeas and chicken absorb all of these flavors together nicely, making this a very well-balanced meal.

Serves 6

3 pounds bone-in chicken thighs

2 teaspoons salt

½ teaspoon black pepper

3 tablespoons olive oil

1 small yellow onion, chopped

2 garlic cloves, minced

2 tablespoons tomato paste

1 medium zucchini, sliced

2 carrots, chopped

2 teaspoons turmeric

3¾ teaspoons Moroccan-spice blend

¾ cup cherry tomatoes

½ cup raisins

⅓ cup chicken broth

1 can (15-ounce) chickpeas, drained and rinsed

2 tablespoons parsley, minced, for garnish

Preheat the oven to 400°F. Season the chicken thighs with 1 teaspoon salt and ¼ teaspoon black pepper. Heat the oil in a Dutch oven over medium heat.

When the oil is hot, add the chicken and sear on both sides for 2 to 3 minutes, just to brown. Transfer the chicken to a plate, then set it aside.

Add the onion and garlic to the same pot and cook for 5 minutes over medium heat. Next, add the tomato paste and cook it for 2 minutes, stirring constantly. Next, add the zucchini and carrots and cook together for 10 minutes. Season the vegetables with turmeric, Moroccan spice blend, and the remaining salt and black pepper, then toss in the cherry tomatoes and raisins.

Add the chicken broth and chickpeas to the pot, then bring the stew to a boil. Next, the chicken thighs in the stew, then cover the Dutch oven and place it in the oven for 25 minutes, or until the chicken is cooked through. Remove the stew from the oven and garnish it with parsley before serving.

Tip: Moroccan spice blend is a combination of classic Moroccan ground spices and can be found in the spice section of most supermarkets and specialty markets.

Chicken & Rice
Casserole

This is what I like to call a no-brainer meal. With just a few common ingredients like rice, chicken, and veggies, this dish comes together baked in the oven. I like thyme in this recipe, but you can certainly substitute thyme for rosemary, oregano, basil, or any combination of herbs for a slight variation.

Serves 2–4

1 cup white or brown rice

2 medium carrots, finely diced

¾ cup broccoli florets

1 cup peas, frozen

2 teaspoons salt, divided

½ teaspoon black pepper, divided

3½ cups chicken broth

2 tablespoons butter

2 boneless skinless chicken breasts

¼ teaspoon dried thyme

Preheat the oven to 375°F. In a bowl, combine the rice, carrots, broccoli florets, and peas and mix well. Pour this into a greased casserole dish and season with a bit of salt and pepper. Pour the chicken broth over the rice and vegetable mixture and dot with butter.

Nest the chicken breasts in the pan with the other ingredients, then season them well with the thyme and the remaining salt and pepper. Cover the pan tightly with foil and bake it in the oven for 50 to 55 minutes, or until the chicken is cooked through. Uncover and serve right out of the casserole dish.

Creamy Garlic Chicken Tri-Colored Pasta Bake

This colorful one-dish wonder comes together effortlessly with the help of tri-colored pasta, chicken, and a quick and easy homemade creamy white sauce. You can make this dish ahead of time if need be and then simply reheat it in the oven before serving. Try this with Gruyère cheese for a more robust flavor.

Serves 2–3

2 cups tri-colored penne pasta

2 tablespoons olive oil

½ medium yellow onion, chopped

3 cloves garlic, minced

½ teaspoon salt

¼ teaspoon black pepper

1 teaspoon dried oregano

1 teaspoon garlic powder

2 tablespoons flour

1½ cups milk

2 cups chicken, diced

1 cup shredded mozzarella cheese

Preheat the oven to 400°F. In a large pot of boiling, salted water, cook the pasta until it's almost completely tender but still has a chew to it. Drain the pasta and set it aside.

Heat a large cast-iron pan over medium heat with olive oil, then add in the onion and garlic and cook for about 10 minutes, or until the onions are tender. Add the salt, pepper, dried oregano, garlic powder, and flour and cook for 5 minutes, stirring continuously. Gradually pour in the milk while whisking to remove any lumps, and bring this mixture to a quick boil. Once it boils, reduce the heat to low and simmer, stirring frequently for 5 more minutes to allow the sauce to thicken up.

Toss in the chicken, mozzarella, and cooked pasta and fold everything together. Place in the oven for 5 to 7 minutes just to thicken the sauce a bit more, and serve hot right out of the cast-iron pan.

CHAPTER TWO

HEARTY BEEF DISHES

The Simplest Beef Stew

Beef stew does something for the soul. It's so satisfying, simple, and delicious, and never seems to fail when I want something hearty and rustic. This recipe includes all the usual suspects like onion, carrot, potatoes, beef sirloin tips, and beef broth. Together these ingredients cook up nicely and create a wonderful meal with everything you need and want in a beef stew. If you're feeling adventurous, you can use sweet potato instead of Yukon golds and can even toss in some cherry tomatoes for added richness.

Serves 6–8

3 tablespoons olive oil, divided

2 medium yellow onions, medium diced

5 large carrots, peeled and cut into large rustic chunks

1 pound small Yukon gold potatoes

5 cloves garlic, peeled and minced

2½ teaspoons salt, divided

1½ teaspoons freshly ground black pepper, divided

4 pounds beef sirloin tips, cut into 1-inch pieces

¼ cup all-purpose flour, divided

2 tablespoons Worcestershire sauce

2 cups beef broth

2 cups water

1 bay leaf

½ teaspoon dried thyme

Heat a large Dutch oven with 2 tablespoons of olive oil to a medium heat. Add the onions and carrots to the pot and cook for 5 to 7 minutes. Next, add the potatoes and garlic and continue to cook all of the vegetables for 10 minutes more, seasoning with ½ teaspoon salt and ½ teaspoon pepper.

Next add the last bit of the oil and let it heat up a bit. While the pan heats up, season the beef with the remaining salt, pepper, and 2 tablespoons of the all-purpose flour and shake off any excess. Place the meat into the hot pan and sear it quickly for about 1 to 2 minutes, then sprinkle the remaining flour over the meat and veggies and mix well while cooking for an additional 1 minute.

Add the Worcestershire sauce and beef broth to the pot and scrape the bottom of the pot to loosen any bits from the bottom. Add the water, bay leaf, and dried thyme and bring the stew up to a boil. Once boiling, turn the heat down and simmer for 10 minutes until the vegetables are fork tender. Taste the stew for seasoning and adjust as necessary. Ladle portions in smaller bowls or individual Dutch ovens and serve warm.

Traditional Lasagna

As cliché as it sounds, I did grow up eating homemade lasagna, and boy was I lucky. My sister would ask for it on her birthday every year and my mom really perfected this dish over the years. Lasagna is very comforting to me and always makes me feel well-fed and happy. It really isn't difficult to prepare—it just takes a little time and some love to make it great.

Serves 8

2 tablespoons olive oil

1 pound ground beef

1 clove garlic, minced

2 teaspoons dried oregano

2 teaspoons dried basil

1½ teaspoons salt

1 teaspoon black pepper

1 medium yellow onion, chopped

1 can (14-ounce) diced tomatoes

1 can (14-ounce) crushed tomatoes

½ teaspoon sugar

2 cups ricotta cheese

1 cup Parmesan cheese, grated and divided

3 tablespoons parsley, minced

1 box lasagna noodles

1 cup mozzarella cheese, grated

Preheat the oven to 350°F. In a large Dutch oven or regular sauté pan, heat the oil to medium. Add the ground beef, garlic, oregano, basil, salt, and pepper, and cook for 5 to 7 minutes or until the beef is nicely browned. Next, add the onion and continue to cook until the onion is tender, then add the diced and crushed tomatoes and the sugar and cook for 10 minutes longer.

In a separate bowl, combine the ricotta cheese and ¾ cup Parmesan cheese with the minced parsley and mix well. In a large pot of boiling, salted water, cook the noodles until they are almost completely tender but still have a chew to them. Drain the pasta and set it aside.

Now begin layering the lasagna. In an oiled 9 x 15-inch casserole dish, spoon 1 cup of sauce into the bottom and spread it evenly. Layer 4 to 5 noodles evenly over the sauce, then top with the cheese mixture, then more sauce and more noodles and continue layering until you've used all of the ingredients, ending with the sauce. Sprinkle the top with mozzarella and the remaining Parmesan cheese. Bake the lasagna for 45 minutes, covered, then uncover it and bake for another 15 minutes just to brown the top. Serve hot out of the oven.

Beef & Mushroom Stew

If you like mushrooms then you will certainly love this dish. Beef & Mushroom Stew is super rich and has an earthy, robust flavor that is irresistible. This recipe calls for button mushrooms, which is really all you need, but if you feel like mixing it up, try a combination of crimini and shiitake mushrooms for a slightly different flavor.

Serves 6–8

2 tablespoons butter

1 tablespoon olive oil

1 pound boneless beef chuck, cubed

2 teaspoons salt, divided

1 teaspoon black pepper, divided

3 cloves garlic, minced

1 large yellow onion, chopped

16 ounces mushrooms, quartered

1 tablespoon tomato paste

2 tablespoons flour

1 teaspoon dried rosemary

½ teaspoon thyme

1 cup red wine

2½ cups beef broth

Heat butter and oil in a large Dutch oven to medium heat. When the pot is hot, add the beef and season with 1 teaspoon salt and ½ teaspoon black pepper, then let the meat sit and cook in the pot without turning or stirring it. After a few minutes, the meat will naturally relax and release from the bottom of the pot. Once it is easy to stir, mix it well to brown it on all sides. Brown the beef for 3 to 4 minutes, then add the garlic and onion to the pot and cook for another

5 minutes. Next, add the mushrooms and tomato paste, season with the remaining salt and pepper, and cook for 5 minutes more, stirring frequently.

Sprinkle the stew with flour, rosemary, and thyme and continue cooking everything for 2 minutes, stirring occasionally until the mixture thickens slightly. Gradually whisk in the wine by scraping the brown bits from the bottom to deglaze it, then add the broth and bring the stew to a boil. Once the stew comes to a boil, reduce the heat to low and simmer uncovered for 45 to 55 minutes or until the meat is completely tender. Before serving, taste the stew and adjust the seasonings as needed.

Shepherd's Pie

You really can't go wrong with this recipe. Ground beef and mixed vegetables sautéed in a flavorful, thick sauce and topped off with fluffy mashed potatoes is a recipe for success. You can also try this exact recipe with ground lamb.

Serves 8

2 tablespoons butter

1 pound ground beef

1½ teaspoons salt, divided

½ teaspoon black pepper, divided

1 clove garlic, minced

1 medium yellow onion, chopped

1 bag (16-ounce) mixed vegetables, frozen

¼ cup parsley, minced

3 tablespoons flour

1½ cups beef broth

4 cups mashed potatoes

Preheat the oven to 400°F. Heat the butter in a large sauté pan over medium heat. Add the beef to the pan and season with ¾ teaspoon salt and ¼ teaspoon pepper. Cook the beef for 3 to 4 minutes just to brown it evenly, breaking up the meat with your wooden spoon as it cooks. Next, add the garlic and onion and cook for 5 to 7 minutes, or until the onions feel soft and tender. Toss in the frozen vegetables and parsley and cook for 2 more minutes.

Sprinkle the flour over the meat and vegetable mix and cook for 2 minutes. Add the beef broth and bring the mixture to a quick boil. Lower the heat to simmer it for 10 minutes, or just until the mixture begins to thicken.

Pour the meat and veggie mixture into an oval cast-iron or regular casserole dish. Spread mashed potatoes evenly over the top, then bake uncovered for 30 minutes, until the potatoes brown slightly on the top.

Beef Stroganoff

Here's another recipe that tastes just as good as it looks and will please anyone it's prepared for. Sirloin steak sautéed in a garlic, onion, and mushroom sauce is good enough as is, but becomes even better with a bit of white wine and beef broth. And as if that wasn't enough, this dish is finished off with silky sour cream to add intense richness.

Serves 4

1 tablespoon butter

2 tablespoons olive oil

1 clove garlic, minced

1 medium yellow onion, finely chopped

2 cups mushrooms, sliced

1½ teaspoons salt, divided

½ teaspoon black pepper, divided

2 teaspoons flour

1 pound beef sirloin steak, cut into strips against the grain

¼ cup white wine

½ cup beef broth

1 teaspoon whole-grain mustard

1 cup sour cream

Heat butter and oil in a large sauté pan over medium heat. Add the garlic and onion and cook for 5 minutes, just until the onion is tender. Next, add the mushrooms and season with ½ teaspoon salt and ¼ teaspoon pepper. Continue to cook for 2 minutes, then add the flour and continue to cook for 2 to 3 more minutes. Meanwhile, cook the pasta in a large pot of boiling salted water until done, then drain and set aside.

Add the beef and the remaining salt and pepper to the pan and cook to brown for 5 minutes. Gradually add the white wine and beef broth while whisking to scrape the brown bits from the bottom to deglaze the pan. Add

the mustard, then bring to a boil. Once boiling, set the heat to LOW and simmer for 10 minutes just until the mixture thickens slightly. Stir in the sour cream, then remove it from the heat and set aside. Serve this over mounds of pasta and enjoy right away.

Beef Noodle Casserole

This recipe is fun to serve because of how delicious it looks when you slice it. Pasta and ground beef together are a great combination that might remind you of the childhood days of Hamburger Helper. This dish has similar charm with a more refined attitude that will please adults and kids simultaneously.

Serves 6–8

2 tablespoons olive oil

10 ounces ground beef

1 teaspoon salt, divided

½ teaspoon black pepper, divided

1 cup carrots, diced

8 ounces penne pasta

4 large eggs

1¼ cups ricotta cheese

1 cup all-purpose flour

2 cups cheddar cheese, grated

Preheat the oven to 350°F. Heat the oil in a sauté pan to medium heat then add the beef, ¾ teaspoon salt, and ¼ teaspoon pepper and cook for 5 minutes to brown the meat. Add the carrots and continue to cook for 5 more minutes, and then set the pan aside to cool. While this mixture cools, cook the pasta in a pot of boiling, salted water, until it is halfway cooked, then drain and set it aside.

In a bowl, combine the eggs, ricotta cheese, flour, and the remaining salt and pepper. Spoon this into a greased casserole dish and sprinkle it with the cheddar cheese. Bake for 35 minutes or until the top is bubbly and browned, then set it aside for 10 minutes before slicing and serving.

Mexican-Style Beef Casserole

It's hard for me to pick favorites, but in this case, it's not that hard. This casserole is definitely at the top of my list because I appreciate and crave the flavors of beans, tomatoes, meat, chili powder, tortillas, and cheese more often than I am willing to admit. I could happily eat this once a week with no complaints, and after making it once, I think you might find yourself falling in love with it too.

Serves 6–8

2 tablespoons olive oil

2 pounds ground beef

1 medium yellow onion, chopped

2 cans (14-ounce each) diced tomatoes

1 can (15-ounce) black beans, drained (1½ cups drained)

2½ teaspoons Mexican-spice blend

½ teaspoon salt

¼ teaspoon black pepper

Corn tortillas

1½ cups cheddar cheese, grated

1½ cups pepper jack cheese, grated

Preheat the oven to 375°F. Heat a sauté pan with the oil to medium, then add the meat and cook it for 5 minutes to brown. Next add the onion and continue to cook for 10 minutes, then add the tomatoes, beans, Mexican spice blend, salt, and black pepper, and cook just until everything is heated through.

Oil a large circular glass baking dish or casserole dish, then arrange one layer of corn tortillas on the bottom, tearing some of the tortillas to make them fit. Cover with half of the meat sauce and half of the cheeses, and then place another layer of tortillas down and top with remaining meat and cheeses.

Bake for 20 to 25 minutes or until the cheese is melted, then let it cool for a few minutes before serving.

Tip: Mexican spice blend is a combination of classic Mexican herbs and spices and can be found in the spice section of most supermarkets and specialty markets.

Beef Cobbler

This recipe is one that will make you appreciate your time in the kitchen. Imagine a delicious and perfect beef stew that is topped off with homemade, buttery cobbler biscuits! Hearty pieces of beef float around in a deliciously flavored beef stew sauce made with onions, celery, garlic, and rosemary. Golden brown biscuits are baked on top and absorb all of the rich flavors of the stew. This dish is perfection.

Serves 8

3 tablespoons olive oil

1 pound flank steak, cubed

2½ teaspoons salt, divided

1 teaspoon black pepper, divided

1 medium yellow onion

1 carrot, chopped

2 stalks celery, chopped

4 cloves garlic, minced

2 cups plus 2 teaspoons all-purpose flour, divided

2 teaspoons dried rosemary

3 cups beef broth

1 tablespoon baking powder

½ cup cold unsalted butter, diced

1 egg, beaten

¾ cup whole milk

Preheat the oven to 425°F. Heat a large Dutch oven to medium heat with oil. Add the meat, 2 teaspoons salt, and ½ teaspoon pepper and cook for 5 minutes to brown the meat. Next, add the onion, carrot, celery, and garlic, and cook for 10 minutes until the vegetables are tender.

Sprinkle the stew with 2 teaspoons of flour and the dried rosemary and continue cooking everything for 2 minutes, stirring occasionally until mixture thickens slightly. Gradually whisk in the beef broth by scraping the brown bits from the bottom to deglaze it, then bring the stew to a boil. Once the stew comes to a boil, reduce the heat to low and set it aside while you make the biscuits.

Combine the last 2 cups of flour with the baking powder, the last ½ teaspoon salt, the last ½ teaspoon pepper, and the butter in a bowl and mix with your fingers until the dough is crumbly. In a separate bowl, beat together the egg and milk and add it to the bowl, mixing well just until a sticky dough ball forms. Transfer the dough to a lightly floured work surface and knead gently, just until the dough comes together. Pat the dough into a disk and cut out rounds with a floured biscuit cutter or cookie cutter, rerolling any leftover dough until you've made all your biscuits. Nest the biscuits in the Dutch oven over the stew and bake in the oven for 22 to 24 minutes, or until the biscuits puff up. Serve warm right away.

Classic Baked Ziti

You can't go wrong with Classic Baked Ziti. The quick homemade tomato sauce with ricotta is tasty and perfect with the ground beef and ziti pasta. These flavors come together nicely in the oven with a blanket of bubbly grated mozzarella to top it all off. If you want a little more goodness, garnish each portion of this dish with a bit of Parmesan cheese when you plate it.

Serves 6–8

16 ounces ziti pasta

2 tablespoons olive oil

4 cloves garlic

1 large onion, chopped

1 pound ground beef

1 can (28-ounce) diced tomatoes

2 cans (15-ounce) tomato sauce

2 teaspoons Italian seasoning

1 teaspoon salt

½ teaspoon black pepper

1 cup ricotta cheese

2 cups mozzarella cheese, grated and divided

Preheat the oven to 350°F. In a large pot of boiling, salted water, cook the pasta until it's almost completely tender but still has a chew to it. Drain the pasta and set it aside.

Heat a sauté pan with oil to medium heat, then add the garlic and onion and cook for 5 minutes until the onion is tender. Add the ground beef and cook for 5 to 7 minutes to brown the meat. Next, add the diced tomatoes, tomato sauce, Italian seasoning, salt, and pepper, and cook for 15 minutes. Let it come together and reduce a bit and then turn off the heat.

Stir the ricotta cheese into the sauce until it blends well, then fold in the pasta and mix well to coat everything. Spoon half of the pasta and sauce mixture into a 9 x 13-inch casserole or baking dish, then layer with a third of the

mozzarella cheese. Next, add the rest of the pasta and sauce and top with the remainder of the grated cheese. Bake in the oven for 30 minutes or until the cheese is bubbly and serve hot right out of the oven.

Tip: Italian seasoning is a combination of classic Italian herbs and spices and can be found in the spice section of most supermarkets and specialty markets.

Baked Potato Gratin with Ground Beef

This recipe is a perfect blend of a classic potato gratin with more body and texture. The ground beef works well here with the potatoes and makes this dish a very filling offering to your meal. You can use potatoes with the skin on for a more rustic feel and to add a bit more color and texture to this dish, although peeling the potatoes makes this a bit more elegant.

2 tablespoons olive oil

1 pound ground beef

1 teaspoon salt, divided

1 teaspoon black pepper, divided

1 small white onion, diced

3 cloves garlic, minced

1 cup sour cream

8 ounces cream cheese

2 cups shredded cheddar cheese, divided

2 pounds russet potatoes, peeled and sliced

3 scallions, minced

Preheat the oven to 400°F. Heat a large sauté pan to medium heat with oil. Add the ground beef, ½ teaspoon salt, ½ teaspoon pepper, and cook for 5 minutes to brown the meat. Next add the onion and garlic and cook for 10 minutes until the onion softens and the meat is cooked through.

In a large mixing bowl, mix together the sour cream, cream cheese, 1 cup cheddar cheese, and the remaining salt and pepper until everything is well combined. Next add the potatoes and meat mixture and mix well.

Grease a 9 x 13-inch casserole dish or baking pan, then pour in the mix-

ture. Sprinkle with the remaining cheddar cheese and cover the gratin with foil. Bake the gratin for 45 to 50 minutes or until the potatoes are tender. Garnish with scallions and serve immediately.

Beef Enchilada Casserole

If you've never made homemade enchiladas, here is a perfect recipe for you to start with. It looks a lot more difficult than it really is, and with everything prepped before you begin to assemble the dish, it will come together in a flash. I like ground beef in this recipe but you certainly can use shredded beef brisket if you want to mix it up.

Serves 6

3 tablespoons olive oil, divided

1 pound ground beef

1 teaspoon salt, divided

1 teaspoon black pepper, divided

1 medium onion, finely diced

3 cloves garlic, minced

2 jalapeños, seeded and minced

1 cup water

1 can (15-ounce) tomato sauce

1 large tomato, diced

1 tablespoon Mexican spice blend

8–10 large corn or flour tortillas

1 cup cheddar cheese, grated

1 cup pepper jack cheese, grated

3 tablespoons parsley, minced

Preheat the oven to 400°F. Heat a sauté pan to medium with 2 tablespoons oil. Add the ground beef, ½ teaspoon salt, and ½ teaspoon pepper and cook for 5 minutes to brown the meat, then set aside.

Add the last tablespoon of oil to another sauté pan. Add the onion, garlic, and jalapeños to the pan and cook for 10 minutes until the onions are tender. Increase the heat and add the water, tomato sauce, and tomato to the pan. Bring this up to a boil for 10 minutes to reduce the sauce, then season with the Mexican spice blend and turn off the heat.

Mix half of the red sauce with the beef and reserve the rest of the sauce in the pan. Wrap the tortillas in a moist paper towel and place them in the microwave for 45 seconds just to steam and make them easier to roll. Combine the cheeses and set them aside to begin to build the enchiladas. Lay a tortilla on a cutting board, fill with a bit of the cheese mixture, add the beef and sauce mixture, and then roll tightly and nest it in a greased 9 x 13-inch casserole dish seam side down. Roll all the rest of the enchiladas until you have used up all of the ingredients, but save about ½ cup of cheese for the top. Pour the remaining red sauce over the enchiladas and sprinkle with the remaining cheese. Cover the casserole dish with foil and bake for 25 minutes, or until the cheese is bubbly. Garnish with parsley before serving.

Hearty Beef & Bean Chili

I have never met anyone who doesn't like a good chili, especially on a cold winter's night. I make chili frequently in my kitchen because it's one of those dishes that I crave on a regular basis. This is a great weeknight meal because it's quick and easy to prepare and can be made ahead of time and reheated with every portion. And the longer it sits the better it gets, so feel free to make this a day or two in advance and serve it up when your guests arrive.

Serves 6–8

3 tablespoons olive oil

2 pounds ground beef

2 teaspoons salt, divided

1 teaspoon black pepper, divided

2 tablespoons Mexican spice blend

1½ cups onion, chopped

4 cloves garlic, minced

1 tablespoon jalapeño, minced

1 cup diced red bell pepper

2 cans (14.5-ounce) diced tomatoes

1 can (15-ounce) kidney beans, drained

Heat a large sauté pan to medium with oil. Add the ground beef, 1 teaspoon salt, and ½ teaspoon pepper, and cook for 10 minutes to brown the meat. Season the meat with the Mexican spice blend and mix well. Next, add the onions, garlic, jalapeño, and bell pepper, and cook for 10 minutes more until the vegetables have softened and the meat is cooked through.

Add the diced tomatoes and the kidney beans and bring the chili to a boil. Once it begins to boil, lower the heat and continue to simmer, covered, for 10 minutes to allow the flavors to come together. Add remaining salt and pepper, taste and adjust the seasoning before serving.

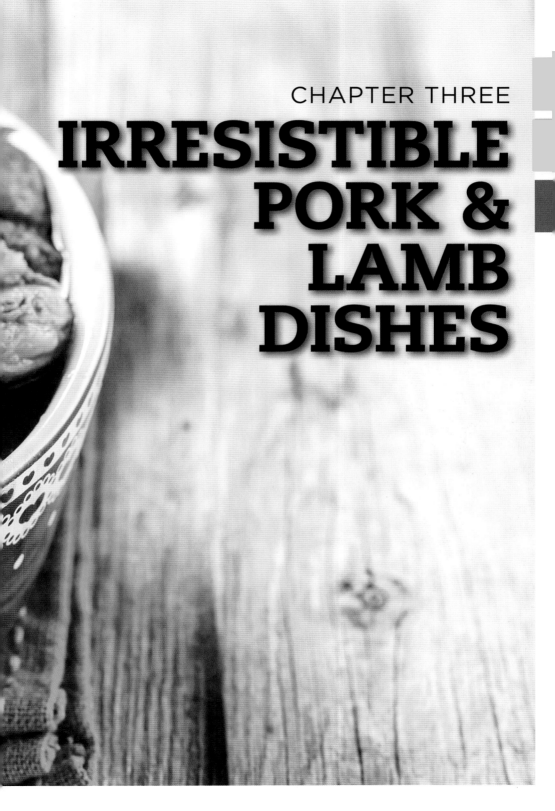

CHAPTER THREE

IRRESISTIBLE PORK & LAMB DISHES

Sausage & Spiral Pasta Casserole

This is a very simple and satisfying recipe that will leave you with dinner in no time. The most time-consuming part about making this dish is preparing the 25-minute tomato and sausage sauce—which is really no time at all considering how flavorful the sauce is. Fusilli pasta is a great noodle for this dish because it helps to absorb and hold the rich and chunky sauce in each bite.

Serves 4

16 ounces fusilli pasta

2 tablespoons olive oil

1 small yellow onion, finely chopped

2 cloves garlic, minced

1 teaspoon salt, divided

½ teaspoon black pepper, divided

2 pounds pork sausage, casings removed

3 teaspoons Italian seasoning

1 can (14.5-ounce) diced fire-roasted tomatoes

1 cup tomato sauce

1½ cups mozzarella, grated

½ cup Parmesan, grated

Preheat the oven to 350°F. In a large pot of boiling, salted water, cook the pasta until it's almost completely tender but still has a chew to it. Drain the pasta and set it aside.

Heat the oil to medium in a large sauté pan, then add the onion and garlic. Season with ½ teaspoon salt and ¼ teaspoon pepper and cook for 10 minutes to soften the onions. Next add the sausage and cook for 5 to 7 minutes, crumbling it in the pan while cooking. Season the meat with the Italian seasoning. Once the meat has browned, add the fire-roasted tomatoes and tomato sauce and season with the remaining salt and pepper. Bring the sauce to a boil, then reduce the heat to low and simmer for 10 minutes. Turn off the heat and add the pasta to the pan along with the mozzarella and mix everything together. Spoon the pasta into a greased casserole dish, sprinkle with Parmesan cheese, and bake in the oven for 15 minutes to heat it through.

Tip: Italian seasoning is a combination of classic Italian herbs and spices and can be found in the spice section of most supermarkets and specialty markets.

Sausage & White Bean Stew

This is one of the best stews I have ever made, and I really can't take credit for it because it's all about how deliciously white beans, sausage, and kale go together. Individually, those three ingredients can do a lot but together they make magic. Make sure to serve this piping hot in big bowls and perhaps even with torn pieces of crusty bread for dipping.

Serves 6-8

2 tablespoons olive oil

3 cloves garlic, minced

1 large yellow onion, chopped

1 teaspoon salt, divided

¼ teaspoon pepper

5 Italian sausage links, prepared and sliced

3 teaspoons herbes de Provence

½ teaspoon red pepper flakes

1 can (14.5-ounce) diced fire-roasted tomatoes

1 can (14.5-ounce) diced tomatoes

1 can (14.5-ounce) white beans, drained

4 cups chicken broth

1½ cups chopped kale

2 tablespoons parsley, minced

Heat the oil in a Dutch oven to medium and then add the garlic and onion. Season with ½ teaspoon salt and all the pepper and cook for 10 minutes to soften the onion. Next, add the sliced sausage and cook for 5 minutes, then season with herbes de Provence, and red pepper flakes.

Next add both the canned tomatoes, white beans, chicken broth, kale, and the remaining salt and bring the mixture to a boil. Once the stew has boiled, reduce the heat to low and simmer for 25 minutes. Before serving, garnish with minced parsley.

Tip: Herbes de Provence is a combination of classic French dried herbs and spices and can be found in the spice section of most supermarkets and specialty markets.

Bacon & Potato
Casserole

Deliciously salty bacon with potatoes is good enough to get your mouth watering before you've even begun cooking this dish. This casserole is perfect for breakfast, brunch, or even as an addition to dinnertime served alongside a few other dishes. I recommend serving breakfast for dinner with this casserole, fried eggs, and a stack of pancakes with berries on the side. It's a real treat that the whole family will love.

Serves 6

Olive oil

1 pound thick-sliced bacon, diced

2 medium yellow onions, chopped

4 cloves garlic, minced

1 teaspoon kosher salt, divided

1 teaspoon black pepper, divided

3 pounds red potatoes, diced

2½ cups Gruyère cheese, grated and divided

Preheat the oven to 400°F. Heat a sauté pan to medium with oil. Add the bacon, onions, and garlic, and then season with ½ teaspoon salt and ½ teaspoon pepper and cook for 10 minutes, until the onions are translucent and the bacon is browned.

In a large bowl, combine the raw, diced potatoes, 1½ cups Gruyère cheese, and the bacon-vegetable mixture and mix until well combined. Season with the remaining salt and pepper, spoon into a greased 9 x 13-inch casserole dish, and sprinkle with the remaining cheese. Cover the dish with foil and bake for 40 to 45 minutes, or until the potatoes are cooked through, and serve.

New Orleans Gumbo

You've got to try this recipe for New Orleans Gumbo. It's a simple and straightforward version of this old classic dish that you can have on the table in just about an hour. Use Andouille sausage for the most authentic version of this recipe, but substitute it for hot Italian sausage if you want to try something with more of a spicy finish.

Serves 6–8

3 tablespoons olive oil

3 cloves garlic, minced

1 medium onion, diced

2 teaspoons salt, divided

½ teaspoon black pepper, divided

1 pound Andouille Sausage, cut crosswise into ¼-inch-thick slices

3 cups okra, sliced

2 stalks celery, diced

1 large bell pepper, diced

1 tablespoon gumbo filé or Creole Spice blend

3 tablespoons butter

3 tablespoons all-purpose flour

8 cups seafood stock

1 can (14.5-ounce) petite-diced tomatoes

2 pounds raw medium shrimp, peeled and deveined (31 to 35 per pound)

2 tablespoons parsley, minced

Heat the oil in a Dutch oven to medium and then add the garlic and onion. Season with 1 teaspoon salt and ¼ teaspoon pepper and cook for 10 minutes to soften the onion. Next add the sausage and cook for 10 minutes more. Next add the okra, celery, and bell pepper and season with gumbo filé and continue to cook for 10 minutes.

Next add the butter and flour to the middle of the pan and mix well, cooking for 2 minutes. Gradually add the seafood stock to the pot while whisking to scrape up the brown bits from the bottom of the pot. Add the tomatoes and bring the gumbo to a boil. Once the gumbo comes to a boil, reduce the heat to low and simmer uncovered for 20 minutes. Add the shrimp and the remaining salt and pepper, and continue to cook the gumbo for 10 minutes more or until the shrimp are evenly cooked. Before serving, taste and adjust the seasoning as needed, then sprinkle with parsley and serve.

Tip: Gumbo filé is a combination of Creole spices and can be found in the spice section of most supermarkets and specialty markets.

Bean & Bacon Stew

As a kid, I would eat a can of Campbell's Bean and Bacon soup every week. Seriously. I didn't skip a week. I loved this soup so much that my parents would buy it in bulk to make sure they had it in the cupboard for me. I haven't had the canned version in years, however, because I have since graduated to this even more delicious homemade version. It's a must try.

Serves 6–8

2 tablespoons olive oil

1 pound bacon, diced

4 cloves garlic, minced

1 medium yellow onion, diced small

3 large carrots, diced small

3 stalks celery, diced small

1 teaspoon salt

½ teaspoon pepper

2 tablespoons tomato paste

½ cup all-purpose flour

8 cups chicken broth

3 cans (15-ounce each) great northern beans, drained (4½ cups drained)

1 bay leaf

Heat a Dutch oven to medium with the oil, then add the bacon, and cook for about 5 to 7 minutes or until the bacon crisps. Remove the bacon from the pot and set aside to drain on a plate with a paper towel. Do not remove the bacon fat from the Dutch oven. Add the garlic, onion, carrots, and celery. Season with the salt and pepper and cook for 10 to 12 minutes or until the vegetables are tender and the onions are translucent. Next add tomato paste and cook for 2 minutes, then mix it into the vegetables. Sprinkle the flour and cook for 2 minutes, then gradually pour in the chicken broth while stirring to scrape up any bits from the bottom of the pot. Add the bacon back to the pot, then add the beans and the bay leaf and bring the stew to a boil. Once it boils, reduce the heat and simmer for 25 minutes. Taste and adjust the seasonings as needed. Remove the bay leaf before serving.

Greek Eggplant Casserole

You can thank the Greeks for this one! Delicious strips of luscious eggplant are layered with a rustic and full-bodied tomato sauce with red wine and ground beef. If we stopped there, that would be enough, but this dish is drizzled with a thick and creamy homemade feta béchamel sauce, and topped with more cheese before browning to golden perfection in the oven. Amen.

Serves 5

2 tablespoons olive oil

3 cloves garlic, minced

1 medium onion, julienned

1 teaspoon salt

½ teaspoon black pepper

1 pound ground beef

¼ cup red wine

3 cans (14.5-ounce each) tomato sauce

1 tablespoon ground oregano

2 teaspoons red pepper flakes

2 eggplants

3 tablespoons butter

3 tablespoons all-purpose flour

1 cup whole milk

¼ cup grated Parmesan cheese

1½ cups feta cheese, crumbled

½ cup mozzarella cheese, grated

Preheat the oven to 375°F. Heat a sauté pan to medium with the oil. Add the garlic and onion and cook for 10 minutes, just until the onions are tender. Season with salt and pepper, then add the beef and continue to cook for 10 minutes to brown the meat. Add the red wine to the pan to deglaze it and cook for another 5 minutes. Next, add the tomato sauce, oregano, and red pepper flakes and bring this to a boil. Once it comes to a boil, reduce the heat to low and simmer for 15 minutes.

Keeping the skin on the eggplant, cut it lengthwise into thin slices. Grease a 9 x 13-inch casserole dish, and then begin layering. Spoon a bit of the meat and sauce mixture into the bottom of the dish and then layer it with slices of eggplant. Top with more sauce, and then another layer of the eggplant slices, and continue layering until the dish is full, then set it aside.

Heat butter in a medium saucepot over medium heat until it's melted, then add the flour and cook for 3 minutes. Gradually whisk in the milk and cook for 5 minutes or until the sauce thickens. Add the Parmesan cheese, feta, and mozzarella to the sauce and mix everything together until the sauce is smooth and the cheeses have melted. Pour the sauce over the casserole dish and bake for 20 minutes until the top is golden brown.

Pasta & Ham Casserole

This is the perfect dish for any time of the year, but is especially perfect for festive celebrations or potlucks with friends. The ham and peas pop in this casserole and make it even more appealing when served to your guests.

Serves 6–8

16 ounces bowtie pasta

3 tablespoons olive oil, divided

5 cloves garlic, minced

1 package (10-ounce) frozen peas

¼ pound thinly sliced country ham, diced small

1 teaspoon salt

½ teaspoon freshly ground pepper

1¼ cups heavy cream

1 cup chicken stock

¼ cup freshly grated Parmesan cheese

¼ cup breadcrumbs

Preheat the oven to 450°F. Bring a stockpot of water to a boil. Once boiling, season the pot with salt and cook the bowtie pasta until they are tender but not overcooked. Drain the pasta, then return them to the pot and toss with 1 tablespoon olive oil to prevent them from sticking.

In a sauté pan, heat the remaining 2 tablespoons olive oil over medium heat. Add the garlic and cook for about 5 minutes. Add the peas and ham and cook until the peas are hot and the ham is lightly browned, about 2 to 3 minutes, then season the pan with salt and pepper. Next, add the cream and the stock and simmer over moderate heat until the sauce is slightly thickened, about 5 minutes. Stir the cream sauce into the bowties. Add the Parmesan and mix well, then spoon everything into your casserole dish.

Top the casserole with breadcrumbs and bake in the oven for 20 minutes, or until the breadcrumbs are just slightly golden brown.

Peppers, Onions, & Sausage Stew

This is a recipe gem. I enjoy taking everyday ingredients and putting them together for something a bit more special. Here we have regular old onions, garlic, bell peppers, and sausages, and they swim together well in a stew of tomatoes and red wine.

Serves 6–8

3 tablespoons olive oil

2 cloves garlic, minced

1 medium yellow onion, sliced

½ teaspoon salt

¼ teaspoon black pepper

1 teaspoon paprika

1 teaspoon dried oregano

2 red bell peppers, chopped

1 yellow pepper, chopped

4 prepared spicy Italian sausages, sliced

1 tablespoon tomato purée

1 cup red wine

1 can (14.5-ounce) chopped tomatoes

Heat a Dutch oven to medium with the oil. Add the garlic and onion and cook for 5 to 7 minutes, just until the onion is tender, and season with salt, pepper, paprika, and oregano. Next add the bell peppers and continue to cook for 5 minutes.

Add the sausages to the pan and cook them for 7 to 10 minutes, until they are browned. Next add the tomato purée and caramelize it in the pan for 3 minutes, then gradually whisk in the red wine to deglaze it and scrape up any brown bits from the bottom. Add the chopped tomatoes and bring the stew to a boil. Once it comes to a boil, reduce the heat to low and simmer for 10 minutes.

Savory Sausage & Potato Breakfast Casserole

Here's a great recipe for your next morning gathering with family and friends. This casserole combines the rich flavors of sausage, eggs, and potatoes and pulls it all together with cheddar and Monterey Jack cheese. Although it's perfect just as it is, you might want to serve this casserole with a dash of hot sauce and sour cream nearby for garnish.

Serves 6

2 tablespoons olive oil

2 cloves garlic, minced

½ cup yellow onion, minced

1 pound ground pork

¼ teaspoon cayenne

1 teaspoon Italian seasoning

1 teaspoon salt, divided

1 teaspoon black pepper, divided

6 eggs

⅓ cup half and half

1½ cups cheddar cheese, grated

4 russet potatoes, peeled and diced

½ cup Monterey Jack cheese, grated

1 tablespoon parsley, minced

Preheat the oven to 400°F. Heat a sauté pan to medium-high with the oil. Add the garlic and onion and cook for 10 minutes, until the onion is tender and caramelized. Next add the ground pork and season it with the cayenne, Italian seasoning, ½ teaspoon salt, and ½ teaspoon pepper. Cook the pork with the onions and garlic for 10 minutes, crumbling it with a wooden spoon as it cooks.

In a mixing bowl whisk together the eggs, half and half, and the cheddar cheese, and season with the remaining salt and pepper. Pour this egg mixture into a greased 9 x 13-inch casserole dish and sprinkle it with the potatoes and the meat mixture. Top with the remaining cheese, cover it with foil, and bake the casserole for 40 to 45 minutes or until the potatoes are tender. Sprinkle it with parsley before serving.

Tip: Italian seasoning is a combination of classic Italian herbs and spices and can be found in the spice section of most supermarkets and specialty markets.

Sausage, Chard, & Pasta Bake

I appreciate this rustic one-pot wonder for its simplicity and sophistication all at the same time. The large rigatoni not only look great in this recipe, but also hold up to the bits of sausage, wilted Swiss chard, and shaved Parmesan. If you feel like mixing it up a bit, you can certainly add tomatoes for color and sweetness, or breadcrumbs on top for added crunch.

16 ounces rigatoni pasta

3 tablespoons olive oil, divided

5 cloves garlic, minced

1 medium onion, chopped

2 cups Swiss chard

1 pound pork sausage links, casings removed

½ teaspoon red pepper flakes

1 teaspoon dried basil

1 teaspoon salt

¼ teaspoon black pepper

½ cup Parmesan cheese, shaved

Preheat the oven to 450°F. Bring a stockpot of water to a boil. Once the water is boiling, season it with salt and cook the pasta until the noodles are tender but not overcooked. Drain the pasta, return them to the pot, and toss with 1 tablespoon olive oil to prevent them from sticking.

In a sauté pan heat the remaining 2 tablespoons olive oil over medium heat. Add the garlic and onion and cook for about 10 minutes, until the onions are translucent. Next add the Swiss chard and cook for 2 to 3 minutes just to wilt it. Add the pork sausage and season with red pepper flakes, basil, salt, and pepper. Cook for 5 to 7 minutes to brown the meat, then add pasta to the pan and toss everything to combine. Bake uncovered for 10 minutes, then remove the pot from the oven and sprinkle it with shaved Parmesan cheese.

Ham & Lentil Stew

I'm pretty sure lentils are my favorite food. I love them and crave them so much that I eat them every few days. As far as I'm concerned, lentils cooked with any pork product is an even more emotional experience. This stew is quite fulfilling in so many ways. The vegetables add depth and richness to the stew and the ham hock adds a savory saltiness that you can't quite get from salt alone.

Serves 6-8

2 tablespoons olive oil

4 cloves garlic, minced

1 large yellow onion, diced small

3 stalks celery, diced small

3 large carrots, diced small

1½ teaspoons salt

½ teaspoon black pepper

1 tablespoon thyme, minced

1 tablespoon rosemary

2 pounds ham hock

1 cup red lentils

1 cup green lentils

4 cups chicken broth

3 cups water

2 bay leaves

Heat a Dutch oven to medium with the oil, then add the garlic, onion, celery, and carrots, and cook or 10 to 12 minutes or until the vegetables are soft. Season the vegetables with salt, pepper, thyme, and rosemary, then add the ham hock and continue to cook for 5 minutes.

Next, add the lentils, chicken broth, water, and bay leaves, and bring the stew to a boil. Once it boils, reduce the heat and simmer it for 50 to 55 minutes.

Remove the ham from the soup and let it cool for 10 minutes. Once the meat is cool enough to touch, slice the meat from the hock, discard the bone, and add the ham meat back to the pot. Taste and adjust the seasoning as needed and remove the bay leaves before serving.

CHAPTER FOUR

FLAVORFUL VEGETABLE & SIDE DISHES

Broccoli & Pepper Egg Casserole

You've got to give this recipe a whirl. Not only is the presentation pretty because of the colors, but the texture and flavor that the vegetables impart on the eggs is craveable and delicious. You can enjoy this casserole any time of day; if you're serving it for dinner, I would suggest pairing it with a hearty salad like a Caesar to satiate you perfectly.

Serves 5–6

2 tablespoons butter

1 clove garlic, minced

½ cup onion, chopped

½ cup chopped red bell pepper

¾ cup broccoli florets

1 teaspoon salt, divided

½ teaspoon pepper, divided

8 large eggs

¼ cup half and half

Preheat the oven to 375°F. Heat a sauté pan to medium with the butter. Add the garlic and onion and cook for 5 minutes, just to soften up the onion. Next add the red bell pepper and broccoli and continue to cook for 5 to 7 minutes. Season the pan with ½ teaspoon salt and ¼ teaspoon pepper and pour the mixture into a buttered round casserole dish.

In a large bowl, beat the eggs and half and half together and season with the remaining salt and pepper. Pour the eggs over the vegetables in the casserole dish and bake the dish in the oven for 25 minutes.

Chickpea & Spinach Stew

This is the easiest and most delicious stew you can make. This Chickpea and Spinach Stew has well-balanced flavors of ginger, garlic, curry, and red pepper flakes. This is a great meal by itself but can be served alongside steamed rice and a green salad for an even heartier meal.

Serves 6–8

3 tablespoons olive oil

1 tablespoon ginger, minced

4 cloves garlic, minced

1 medium yellow onion, minced

1 teaspoon salt

½ teaspoon black pepper

1 tablespoon curry powder

¼ teaspoon red pepper flakes

1 can (15-ounce) tomato sauce

1 can (29-ounce) chickpeas, drained

1 cup baby spinach

Heat the oil in a Dutch oven to medium, then add the ginger, garlic, and onion and cook for 10 minutes, just to soften up the onion. Season with the salt, pepper, curry powder, and red pepper flakes. Add the tomato sauce and chickpeas and bring the stew to a boil. Once it boils, add the spinach and lower the heat to simmer for 20 minutes. Before serving, taste and adjust the seasonings as needed.

Corn Chowder

Corn chowder is one of my favorite ways to use frozen corn. This recipe is rich and delicious, and doesn't cut corners when it comes to flavor. The potatoes add an interesting thickness to the chowder and the half and half adds a silky, creamy texture that makes this dish irresistible. It is best enjoyed right after you've made it.

Serves 6–8

2 tablespoons butter

2 cloves garlic, minced

1 medium yellow onion, diced

1 teaspoon salt, divided

½ teaspoon black pepper, divided

2 large russet potatoes, diced

2 tablespoons flour

2 cups chicken broth

2 cups half and half

2 bags (10 ounces each) fire-roasted frozen corn

Heat the butter in a Dutch oven to medium, then add the garlic and onion and cook for 10 minutes, just to soften up the onion. Season with ½ teaspoon salt and ¼ teaspoon pepper, then stir well and add the potatoes, and continue to cook for 5 to 7 minutes to soften them up.

Sprinkle the flour over the vegetables and cook for 2 to 3 minutes, then gradually add the chicken broth while whisking to scrape up any of the brown bits from the bottom of the pot. Add the half and half and bring the chowder to a boil. Once it boils, add the corn and lower the heat to a simmer for 20 minutes.

Quickly purée the chowder using an immersion or regular blender, then add it back to the pot and warm again as needed. Taste and adjust the seasonings before serving.

Red Lentil Stew

Red lentils are so delicious in stews because they tend to fall apart and add to the richness and thickness of any recipe. In this case, sweet potatoes and carrots pair well with the lentils to create a sweet and savory flavor combination. The red pepper flakes and hot curry powder can be substituted for milder ingredients if you'd prefer less zip to your stew.

Serves 4–6

3 tablespoons olive oil

4 cloves garlic, minced

1 medium yellow onion, diced medium

2 sweet potatoes, peeled and diced medium

1 carrot, peeled and diced medium

1 teaspoon salt

½ teaspoon dried red pepper flakes

1 can (28-ounce) diced tomatoes, drained

1 teaspoon paprika

½ teaspoon hot curry powder

1 cup red lentils

4 cups vegetable broth

2 cups water

Freshly ground black pepper

Juice of ½ lemon, to taste

Heat a large stockpot with olive oil to medium heat. Add the garlic and onion to the pot and cook for 5 to 7 minutes. Next add the sweet potatoes and carrot and continue to cook all of the veggies for 5 to 7 minutes. Season the pot with the salt and red pepper flakes.

Next add the diced tomatoes to the pot and season with the paprika and hot curry powder. Add the red lentils, vegetable broth, and water, and bring the soup up to a rapid boil. Once the soup boils, lower the heat and continue to cook on a simmer for 10 to 15 minutes, until the lentils and vegetables are tender.

Taste the stew for seasonings and adjust as necessary. Serve warm right away with freshly ground pepper and a squeeze of lemon added to each bowl.

Macaroni & Cheese Bake

Elbow macaroni—drenched in a homemade cheese sauce and baked in the oven with a bit more cheese on top—makes this dish an all-around favorite of many. You can try using different types of cheeses for variations in flavor, such as a combination of Gruyère and Parmesan for a more unique and refined taste.

Serves 6–8

16 ounces elbow macaroni

½ cup butter

½ cup all-purpose flour

5 cups milk

1½ teaspoons dry mustard

⅛ teaspoon paprika

⅛ teaspoon ground nutmeg

½ teaspoon kosher salt

1½ cups Romano cheese, grated

4½ cups cheddar cheese, grated and divided

Preheat the oven to 375°F. In a large pot of boiling, salted water, cook the pasta until it's almost completely tender but still has a chew to it. Drain the pasta and set it aside.

Add the butter to a large stockpot over medium heat. Once the butter melts, whisk in the flour and let this mixture cook for 5 minutes, stirring constantly. Gradually add the milk while whisking and continue to cook for 5 minutes, until the sauce thickens. Add the dry mustard, paprika, nutmeg, salt, Romano cheese, and 3½ cups of the cheddar cheese. Stir everything together until the cheese melts and the sauce is smooth, then turn off the heat.

Add the pasta to the sauce and fold everything together to coat it evenly. Spoon the pasta into a 3-quart buttered casserole dish. Top the dish with the remaining cup of cheddar cheese and then bake for 25 minutes, or until the cheese melts and turns slightly golden brown on the top.

Green Bean Casserole

This has been a holiday staple in my family for as long as I have had any say in the meal. I really appreciate a good green bean casserole for its multitude of flavors and texture, including woody mushrooms, creamy mushroom soup, the freshness of the green beans, the saltiness from the cheese, and the crunch from the French-fried onions. This dish is best made right before serving for the liveliest-tasting casserole.

Serves 5–6

2 cups chicken broth

4 cups green beans, ends trimmed and halved

2 tablespoons butter

1 cup sliced mushrooms

1 can (10.75-ounce) condensed cream of mushroom soup

⅓ cup milk

1 teaspoon Worcestershire sauce

1½ cups shredded cheddar cheese

2 cups French-fried onions, divided

Preheat the oven to 350°F. Combine the chicken broth and green beans in a sauté pan. Bring them to a boil, then reduce the heat and simmer for 5 minutes, just to soften the green beans. Then drain the beans and set them aside in a mixing bowl.

Add the butter to the same pan and heat over medium. Add the mushrooms and cook for 5 minutes just to brown them. Add the mushrooms to the green beans and add the condensed cream of mushroom soup, milk, Worcestershire sauce, cheddar, and ½ cup French-fried onions. Spoon this mixture into a greased 1½-quart casserole dish, sprinkle with the remaining onions, and bake in the oven for 25 minutes or just until the casserole is hot and bubbly.

Asparagus Egg Bake

This recipe takes a few simple ingredients and makes them feel a lot more sophisticated. It's important to use real cream and regular goat cheese in this recipe for the creamiest and fullest flavor possible. The eggs will thank you for that once you have a taste. Also, try and pick the best-looking asparagus to show off in this dish. They will not only taste the best but will also stand up the best once baked.

Serves 5

2 tablespoons olive oil

2 cloves garlic, minced

1 leek, sliced

1 teaspoon salt, divided

½ teaspoon black pepper, divided

12 eggs

2 tablespoons heavy cream

2 teaspoons Italian seasoning

2 cups Yukon gold potatoes, sliced

1 pound fresh asparagus, ends trimmed and cut into 1-inch pieces

4 ounces goat cheese

Preheat the oven to 375°F. Heat a sauté pan to medium with the oil. Add the garlic and the leek to the pan and cook for 5 to 7 minutes. Season with ½ teaspoon salt and ¼ teaspoon pepper, then remove the pan from the heat and set aside.

In a large bowl, beat together the eggs, cream, and Italian seasoning. Add the remaining salt and black pepper. Pour the mixture into a well-buttered circular casserole dish, and then sprinkle it with the potatoes, asparagus, and goat cheese. Bake for 35 to 40 minutes, until the eggs are well set and the potatoes are tender.

Tip: Italian seasoning is a combination of classic Italian herbs and spices and can be found in the spice section of most supermarkets and specialty markets.

Vegetable Bread Pudding

Bread pudding is so delicious and comforting. Most of us have had many types of the sweet variation, but this dish is on the opposite end of the flavor spectrum, showcasing the flavors of earthy zucchini and bell peppers along with cheesy mozzarella and tangy sourdough bread. This dish is similar to a stuffing, but with much larger pieces of ingredients floating around in a cooked egg, milk, and bread mixture.

Serves 6–8

2 tablespoons olive oil

6 cups sourdough baguette, cubed

1 shallot, chopped

3 cloves garlic, minced

1 large zucchini, chopped

1 red bell pepper, chopped

1 green bell pepper, chopped

4 scallions, minced

6 large eggs

2 cups milk

¼ teaspoon dried thyme

1 cup mozzarella cheese, grated

1 teaspoon salt

¾ teaspoon black pepper

Preheat the oven to 350°F. Oil a 2-quart casserole dish and then layer it with half the bread cubes. Next add half of the shallot, garlic, zucchini, bell peppers, and scallions, and layer each vegetable evenly in the casserole dish. Finish with another layer of bread and the rest of the vegetables.

Whisk together the egg, milk, thyme, and mozzarella cheese and mix well.

Pour the egg mixture over the vegetables and bread and season it evenly with salt and pepper. Cover the dish with foil and chill it in the refrigerator for 2 hours. Keeping it covered, bake the casserole for 45 to 50 minutes.

Parsnip Gratin

Parsnips are such an underutilized ingredient these days. I didn't grow up eating parsnips, but really started to integrate them into my recipes and cooking after I learned how delicious they were while I was working in restaurants. I like the versatility of this vegetable and really enjoy emphasizing its distinctive flavor in this gratin. The milk and cheeses really enhance the parsnip flavor and make it even more enjoyable than it already is on its own.

Serves 5–6

- 1 tablespoon butter
- 2 tablespoons all-purpose flour
- 1½ cups milk
- 2 cups Parmesan cheese, grated and divided
- 2 teaspoons fresh thyme, chopped
- 1 teaspoon salt
- ¼ teaspoon black pepper
- 4 parsnips, peeled and chopped
- ½ cup Gruyère cheese, grated

Preheat the oven to 350°F. Heat a saucepan to medium and add the butter and flour, whisking to combine. Gradually pour in the milk while whisking to remove all the lumps. Continue to whisk for 2 to 3 minutes, just until the sauce begins to thicken, then remove the pan from the heat and add 1 cup Parmesan cheese as well as the thyme, salt, and pepper.

Spoon a layer of the sauce into the bottom of a buttered, round 8-inch casserole dish, then add the parsnips to the dish. Spread the parsnips so that they are all lying flat, then pour the remaining sauce over the top and sprinkle with the remaining cheeses. Bake for 45 minutes or until the top is golden brown, then remove the gratin from the oven and serve immediately.

Eggplant Parmesan Bake

Eggplant Parmesan is such a filling dish that is adored by so many people, especially people who love casseroles with a lot of sauce and layers. If you like lasagna then you will love this too. The sauce in this recipe is simple and classic and is updated just slightly with fresh oregano and basil. Layering this dish only takes a few minutes, but keep in mind that you can build this ahead of time and bake it right before you want to serve for the most inviting, piping-hot look.

Serves 8

2 tablespoons olive oil

4 cloves garlic, minced

1 tablespoon tomato paste

¾ teaspoon salt, divided

¼ teaspoon pepper

⅛ teaspoon red pepper flakes

2¼ cups tomato sauce

1 cup water

½ teaspoon oregano

5 basil leaves, chopped

3 eggplants

1 cup mozzarella, grated

1 cup cheddar cheese, grated

¾ cup Parmesan cheese

Preheat the oven to 350°F. Heat a sauté pan with the olive oil on medium-low heat. Add the garlic and tomato paste to the pan and cook for 5 minutes. Season with ½ teaspoon salt, the pepper, and the red pepper flakes. Next, add the tomato sauce, water, oregano, and basil, and bring the sauce to a boil. Once it boils, lower the heat and bring it to a simmer for 15 minutes.

While the sauce cooks, slice the eggplants lengthwise into thin slices with the skin left on. Oil a 9 x 13-inch baking dish and spoon a bit of sauce evenly over the bottom of the dish. Layer the eggplant evenly in the dish, then spoon sauce on top and sprinkle it with a bit of the mozzarella and cheddar cheese. Continue with more layers of eggplant, sauce, and cheese until the baking dish is full. Sprinkle the top with Parmesan cheese and bake for 25 to 30 minutes, or until the cheese is bubbly, and serve hot right out of the oven.

Cheesy Scalloped Potatoes

These Cheesy Scalloped Potatoes will be eaten faster than you can make a batch. I don't know why but most people go crazy for the combination of potatoes and cheese, and this recipe does it especially well. The combination of white cheddar and Gruyère cheese is tangy and creamy and will leave your taste buds smiling while doing cartwheels.

Serves 6–8

- 5 tablespoons butter
- 5 tablespoons all-purpose flour
- 3 cups milk
- 2 teaspoons salt
- ½ teaspoon black pepper
- 1 teaspoon paprika
- 1½ cups white cheddar cheese, grated and divided
- 1½ cups Gruyère cheese, grated and divided
- 5 large russet potatoes, sliced
- 2 tablespoons minced parsley

Preheat the oven to 375°F. In a sauté pan, heat the butter on medium. Once the butter is melted, add the flour and whisk slowly and continuously for 2 to 3 minutes. Gradually add the milk a little at a time and whisk to remove all of the lumps. Lower the heat to a low flame and continue to cook for 5 minutes to thicken the sauce, whisking frequently. Remove the pan from the heat and then season it with salt, pepper, and paprika and stir in 1 cup of the cheddar cheese and 1 cup of the Gruyère cheese.

Add half of the potatoes to a buttered 9 x 13-inch casserole dish. Spoon half of the cheese sauce over the potatoes, then add the remaining potatoes and the rest of the sauce. Sprinkle the top with the rest of the cheddar and Gruyère cheese and bake in the oven for 40 to 45 minutes, until the potatoes are tender and the cheese is bubbly and golden brown on top. Remove the dish from the oven and garnish with minced parsley before serving.

Pasta & Broccoli Casserole

Here's another casserole crowd-pleaser that you and your family will adore. Pasta and broccoli make magic together when they are baked in a pool of homemade cheddar sauce and topped with crispy breadcrumbs for texture and crunch. The colors pop in the dish and the flavors will pop in your mouth.

Serves 8

3 cups elbow macaroni

4 cups broccoli florets

½ cup butter

3 tablespoons all-purpose flour

½ teaspoon garlic powder

½ teaspoon onion powder

¾ teaspoon salt

¼ teaspoon pepper

2 cups heavy cream

2½ cups cheddar cheese, grated and divided

½ cup coarse breadcrumbs

Preheat the oven to 375°F. In a large pot of boiling, salted water, cook the pasta for 5 minutes, then add the broccoli florets and cook for 3 to 5 more minutes until the pasta and broccoli are almost completely tender but still have a slight chew to them. Drain the pasta and broccoli and set them aside.

Add the butter to a stockpot over medium heat. Once the butter melts, whisk in the flour, garlic powder, onion powder, salt, and pepper, and cook for 5 minutes, stirring frequently. Gradually whisk in the heavy cream to remove the lumps, then bring this mixture to a boil. Once it boils, lower the heat and simmer it for 3 to 4 minutes to thicken it, and then stir in 2 cups cheese.

Add the pasta and broccoli to the sauce and fold everything together to

coat it evenly. Spoon the pasta into a buttered 3-quart casserole dish and sprinkle the top evenly with the remaining cheddar cheese and breadcrumbs. Bake the dish in the oven for 25 minutes or until the cheese melts and turns slightly golden brown on the top.

Zucchini & Cheese Casserole

There's nothing like fresh zucchini sautéed with garlic to make your kitchen smell like home cooking. Keep the skin on the zucchini for added crunch and color in this dish. You can make the sauce with cheddar or jack cheese, although I like the creamy consistency and color of cheddar a bit more with the green of the zucchini. Don't forget to top your casserole with minced green onions right before you serve to add even more color and intrigue to this dish.

Serves 5–6

2 tablespoons olive oil

5 cloves garlic, minced

5 medium zucchini, sliced

½ teaspoon salt, divided

¼ teaspoon black pepper

2 cans (12-ounce each) evaporated milk

2 cups grated cheddar cheese

3 green onions, minced

Preheat the oven to 375°F. Heat a sauté pan with olive oil to medium heat. Add the garlic and zucchini to the pan and cook for 5 to 7 minutes, or until the zucchini is softened. Season with ¼ teaspoon of the salt and the pepper, then remove the pan from the heat and add this mixture to a greased casserole or baking dish

Heat the sauté pan again, then add the evaporated milk and bring it to a boil. Once it boils, lower the heat to a simmer and season it with the remaining salt. Stir in 1½ cups of the cheddar cheese and mix until the sauce is smooth. Pour the sauce over the zucchini and garlic mixture, sprinkle it with the remaining cheese, and bake it for 20 to 25 minutes or until top is golden brown. Sprinkle it with minced green onions before serving.

Index

Page numbers in italics indicate illustrations.